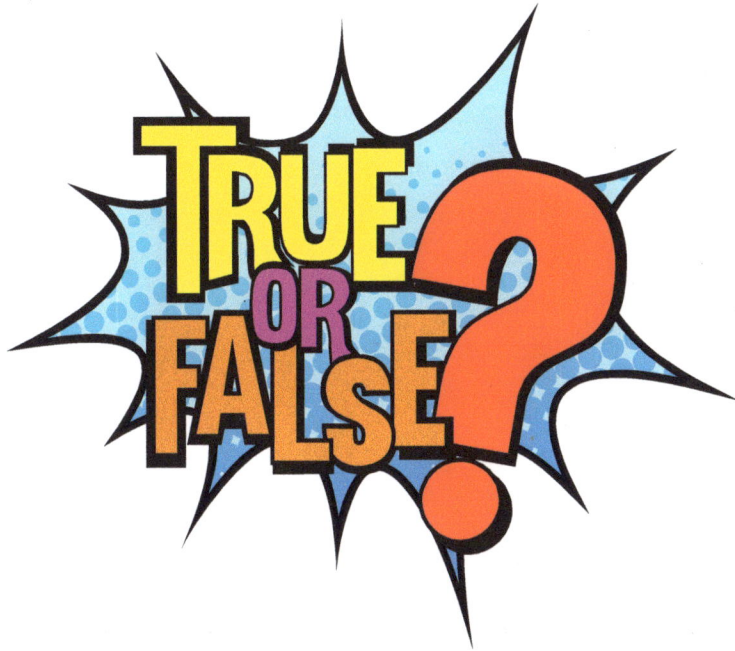

Co-published by agreement between Shi Tu Hui and World Book, Inc.

Shi Tu Hui
Room 1807, Block 1,
#3 West Dawang Road
Chaoyang District, Beijing 100025
P.R. China

World Book, Inc.
180 North LaSalle Street
Suite 900
Chicago, Illinois 60601
USA

Library of Congress Cataloging-in-Publication Data for this volume has been applied for.

True or False? (set #4)
ISBN: 978-0-7166-5417-9 (set, hc.)

Animation
ISBN: 978-0-7166-5419-3 (hc.)

Also available as:
ISBN: 978-0-7166-5429-2 (e-book)
ISBN: 978-0-7166-5439-1 (soft cover)

Staff

Executive Committee

President
Geoff Broderick

Vice President, Editorial
Tom Evans

Vice President, Finance
Molly Stedron

Vice President, International and Marketing
Eddy Kisman

Vice President, Technology and Operations
Jason Dole

Director, Human Resources
Bev Ecker

Editorial

Writer
Fred Maxon

Manager, New Content
Jeff De La Rosa

Associate Manager, New Content
William D. Adams

Curriculum Designer
Caroline Davidson

Proofreader
Nathalie Strassheim

Graphics and Design

Coordinator, Design Development & Production:
Brenda Tropinski

Senior Visual Communications Designer
Melanie Bender

Senior Media Editor
Rosalia Bledsoe

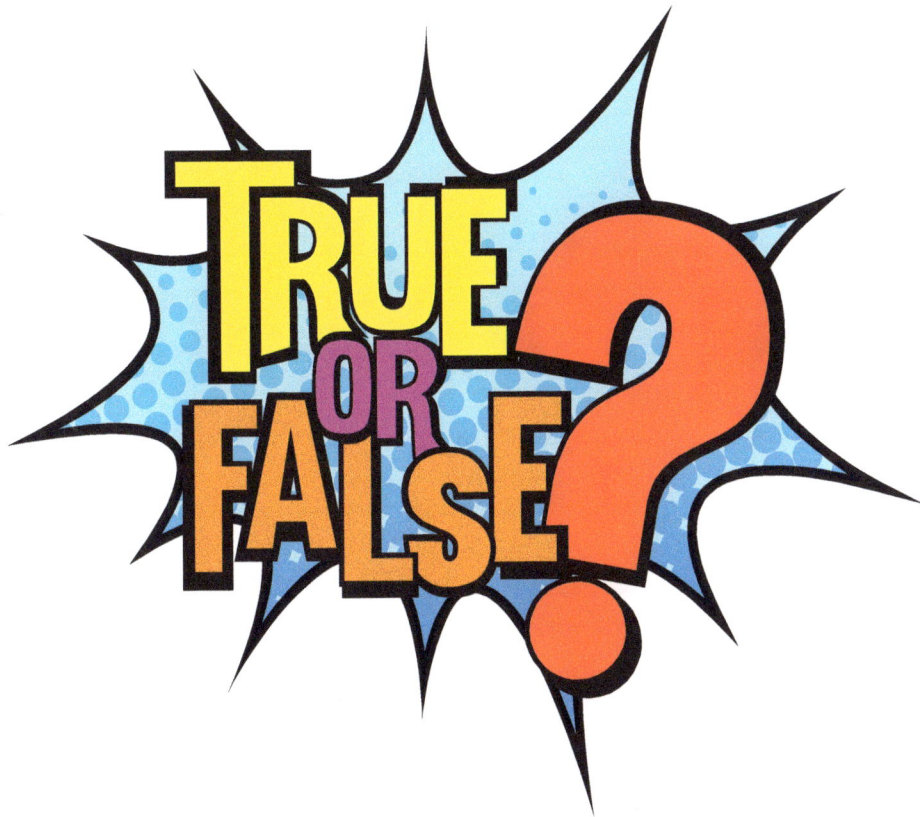

TRUE OR FALSE?

ANIMATION

WORLD
BOOK

www.worldbook.com

TRUE OR FALSE?

Walt Disney accidentally invented animation in 1925, when he drew on a film he was making.

FALSE!

Animation has been around longer than you might think. Some of the earliest motion pictures made use of animation in the late 1800's and early 1900's. Even before that, devices called *magic lanterns* used quickly flickering drawings to create the illusion of moving images.

TRUE OR FALSE?

The animated television series "Peppa Pig" was created by three friends who were out of work.

TRUE!

(snort) The animators Neville Astley and Mark Baker and the producer Phil Davies borrowed money from friends and family to create the lovable Peppa. She first appeared on television in the United Kingdom in 2004.

TRUE OR FALSE?

The character Mickey Mouse first appeared in the 1931 animated short film *Mitchell Mouse Gets Married.*

FALSE!

Mickey Mouse first appeared (with Minnie Mouse) in the 1928 short film *Steamboat Willie.* It was the first animated film to have a *synchronized* soundtrack—that is, sound matched up with the action on screen.

TRUE OR FALSE?

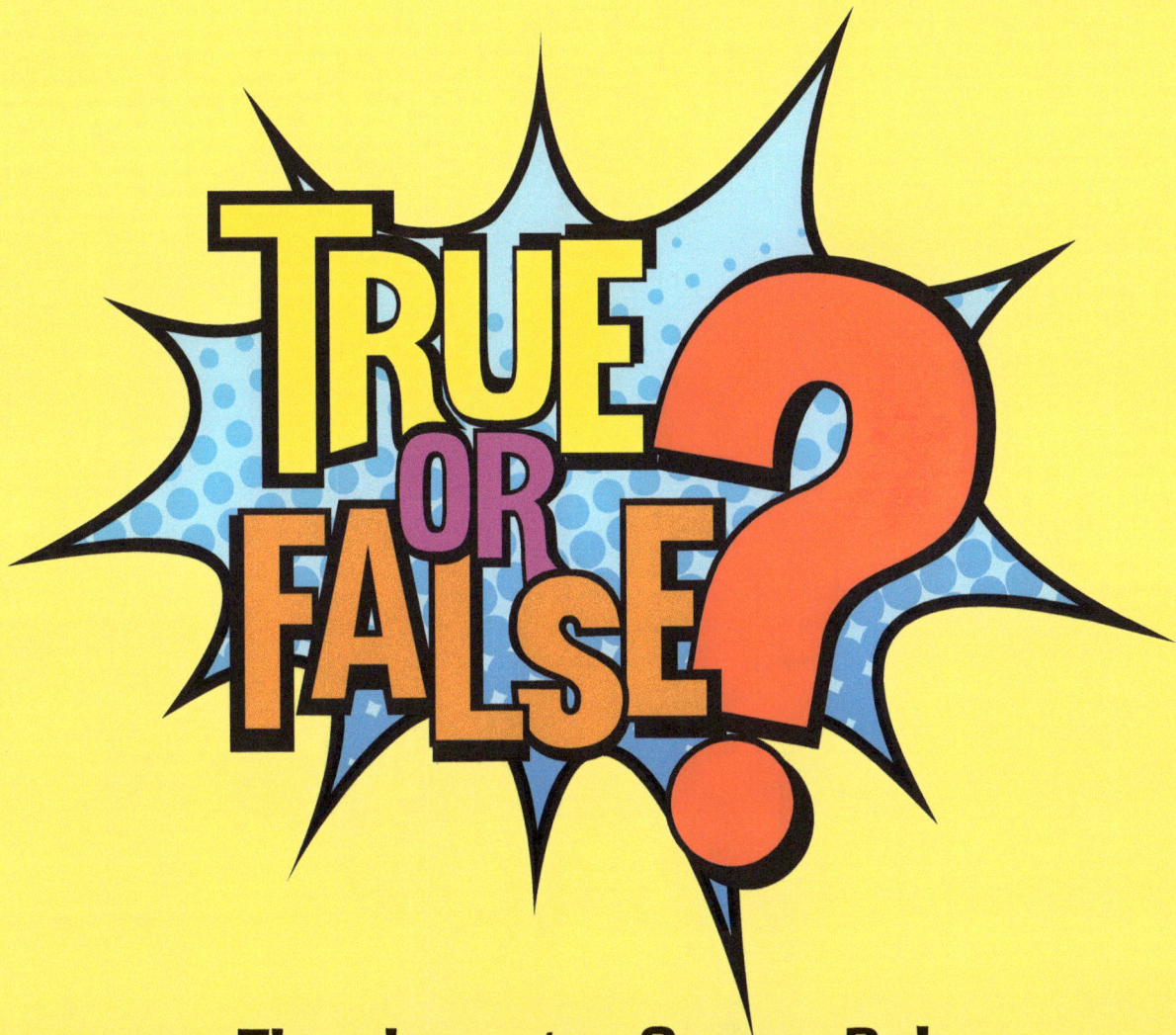

The character SpongeBob Squarepants was created by a former marine biology professor, who doodled different sea creatures on his handouts.

TRUE!

Before he became an animator, Stephen Hillenburg taught *marine biology*—the study of sea life—at the Ocean Institute in Dana Point, California. Hillenburg went on to create the television series "SpongeBob Squarepants" in 1999.

TRUE OR FALSE?

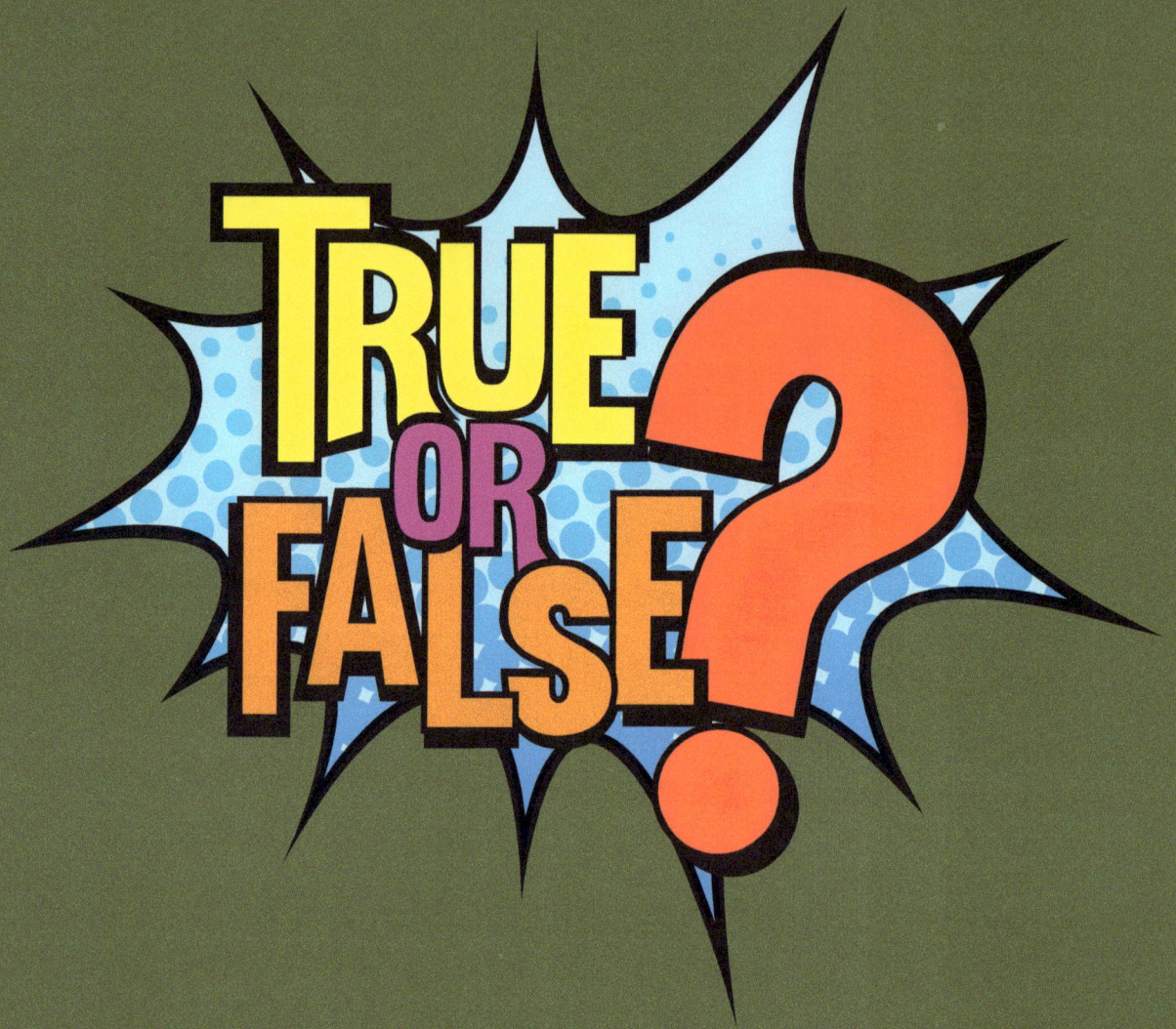

The character Bugs Bunny got his name because he was always "bugging" the hapless hunter Elmer Fudd.

FALSE!

Bugs Bunny was named after an animator at the Warner Bros. entertainment studio, where the character was created. Ben "Bugs" Hardaway was one of the artists who first drew the rabbit for the 1938 cartoon "Porky's Hare Hunt."

TRUE OR FALSE?

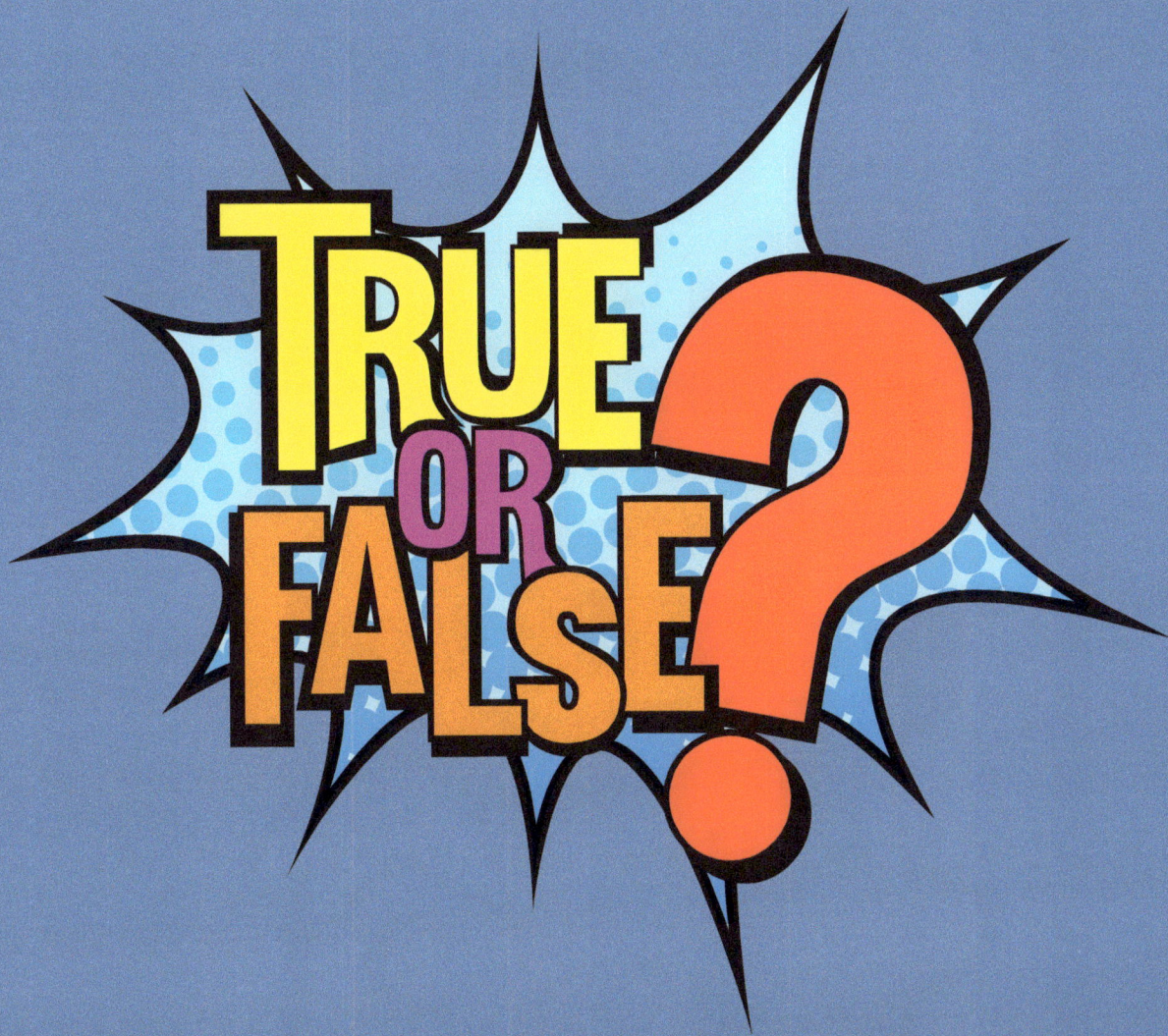

Mel Blanc, who provided the voice of Bugs Bunny, also voiced the characters Yosemite Sam, Pepe LePew, Porky Pig, and Daffy Duck.

TRUE!

Blanc voiced many of the most popular characters from the Warner Bros. animation studio. In the 1960's, he became the voice of Barney Rubble on the animated television series "The Flintstones."

TRUE OR FALSE?

The style of animation called *anime* was invented by the American illustrator Annie-Mae Jones.

29

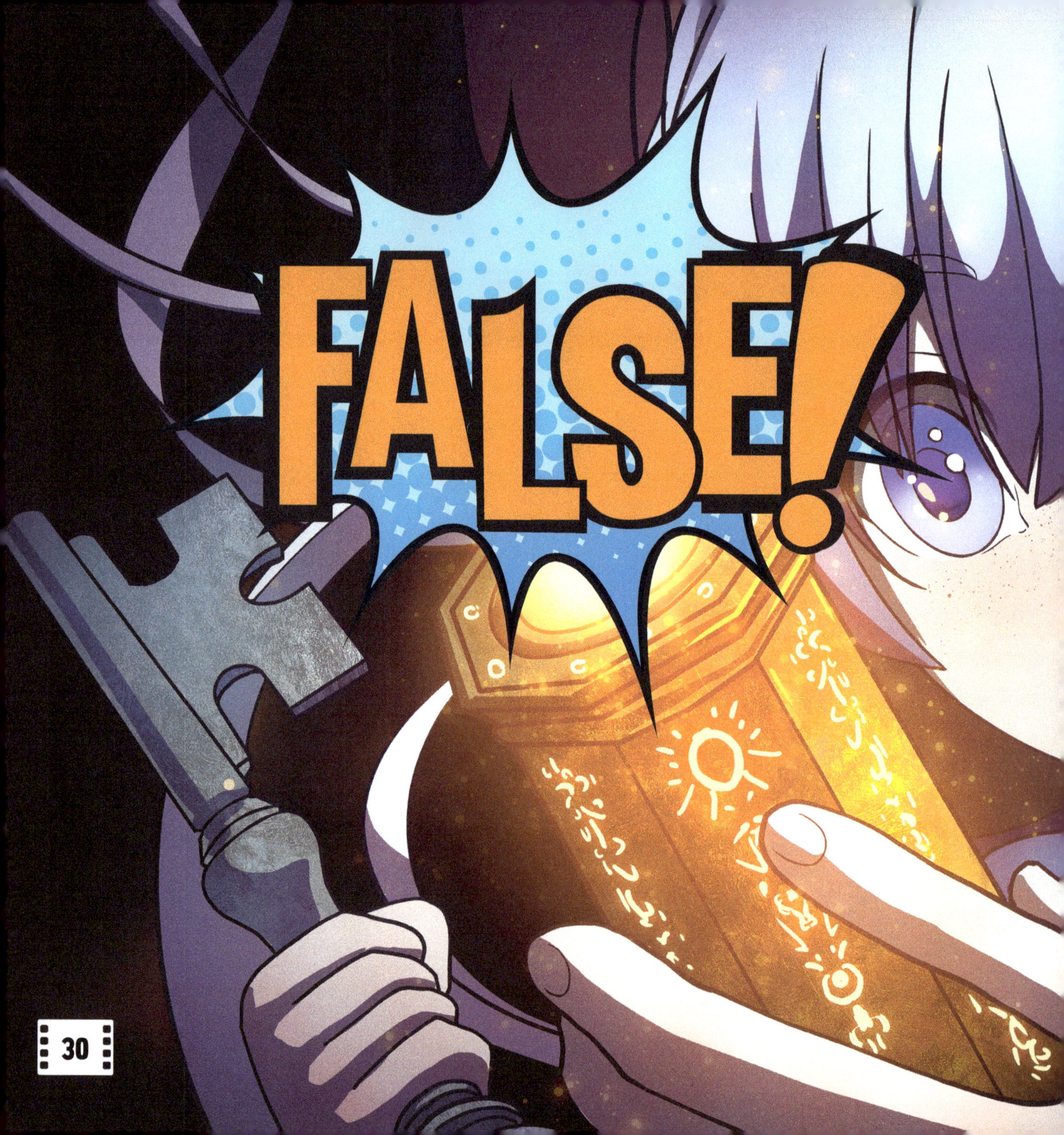
FALSE!

Anime is a Japanese style of animation that has roots in the early 1900's. Many distinctive features of modern anime—including big-eyed characters and the combination of still and moving images—came about during the 1960's.

TRUE OR FALSE?

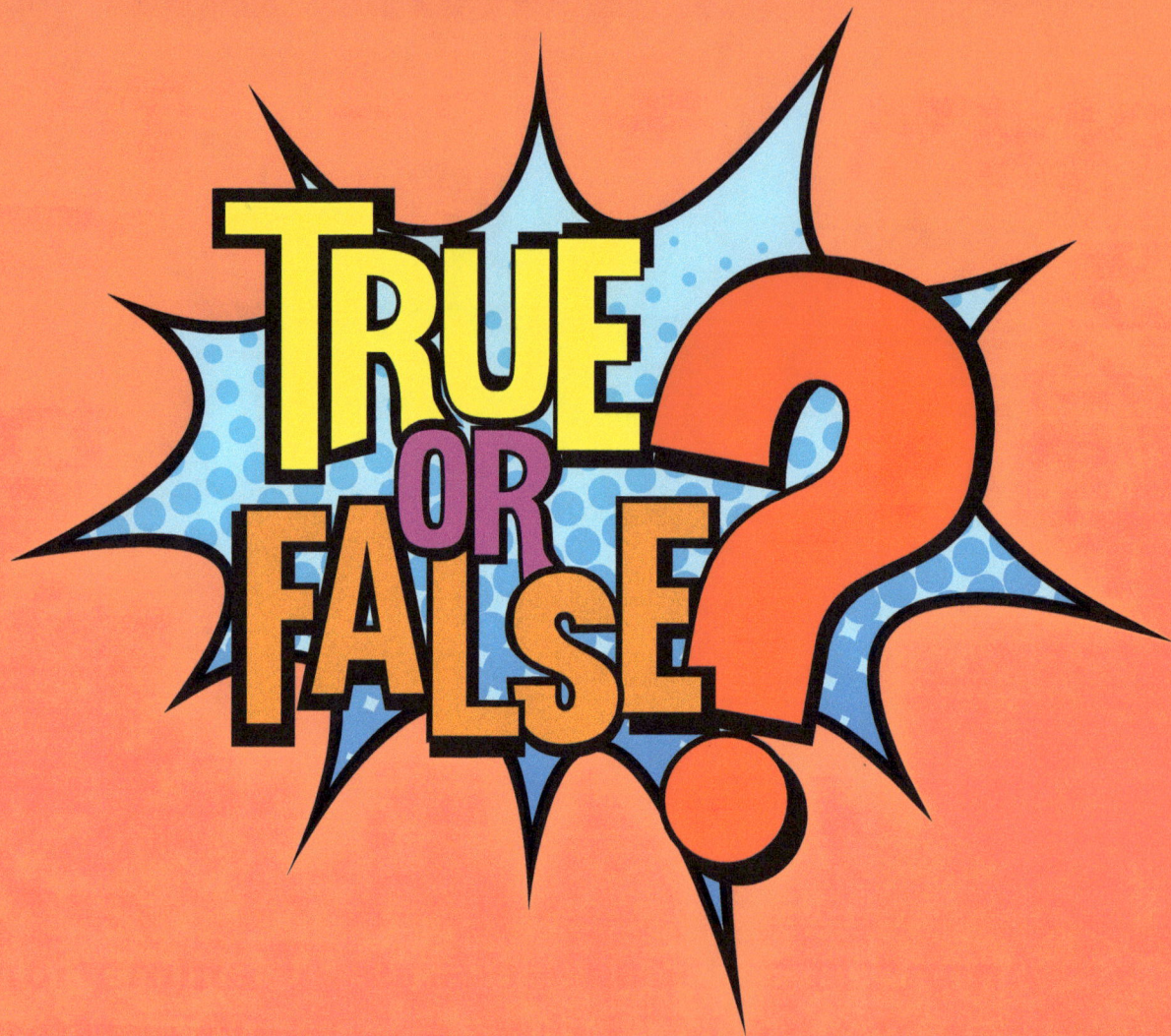

The animated motion picture *Snow White and the Seven Dwarfs* (1938) was so beloved that Walt Disney won a special Academy Award for it.

TRUE!

Snow White and the Seven Dwarfs was not nominated in any particular category. But, Disney was given a special award—and seven miniature awards—for the film. Shirley Temple, a popular child star of the 1930's, presented Disney with the eight statuettes.

TRUE OR FALSE?

Even though *Snow White and the Seven Dwarfs* is an animated movie, the animator Walt Disney had actual sets built and costumes made for it.

TRUE!

The American actress and dancer Marge Champion acted out many of the scenes in *Snow White* on set and in full costume. Then, animators traced over the footage. This technique is called *rotoscoping*.

TRUE OR FALSE?

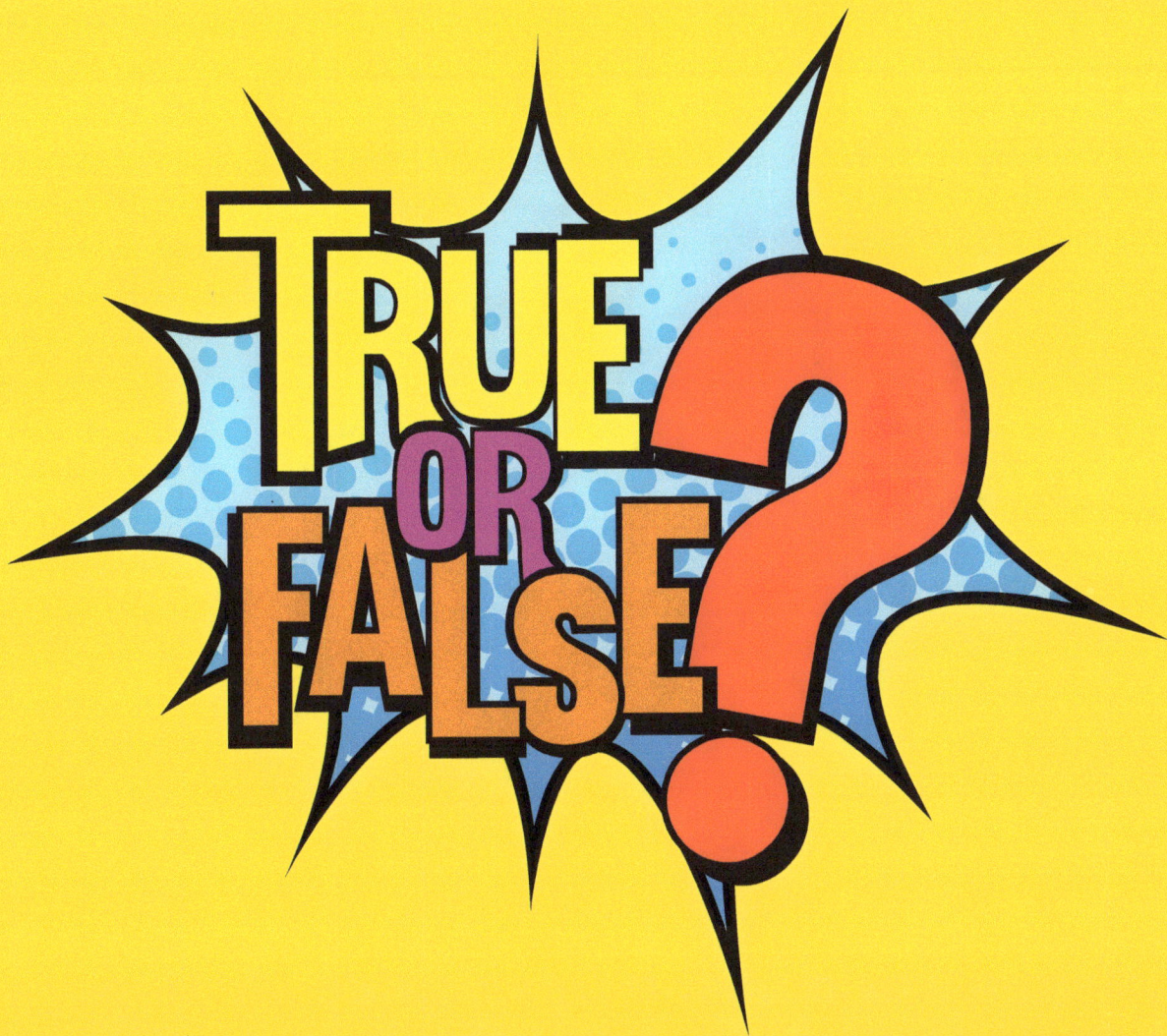

The lovable yellow characters known as Minions were first introduced in the animated motion picture *Despicable Me* (2010).

TRUE!

In the world of the *Despicable Me* films, Minions are some of the oldest surviving creatures, remaining relatively unchanged for over 60 million years. The 2015 film *Minions* shows them serving a *Tyrannosaurus rex.*

TRUE OR FALSE?

Animators voiced the Minions by editing together bird calls, cats meowing, and the French language.

FALSE!

The directors of the *Despicable Me* films, Pierre Coffin and Chris Renaud, provided their voices for the Minions. The voices were altered by computer to sound higher.

TRUE OR FALSE?

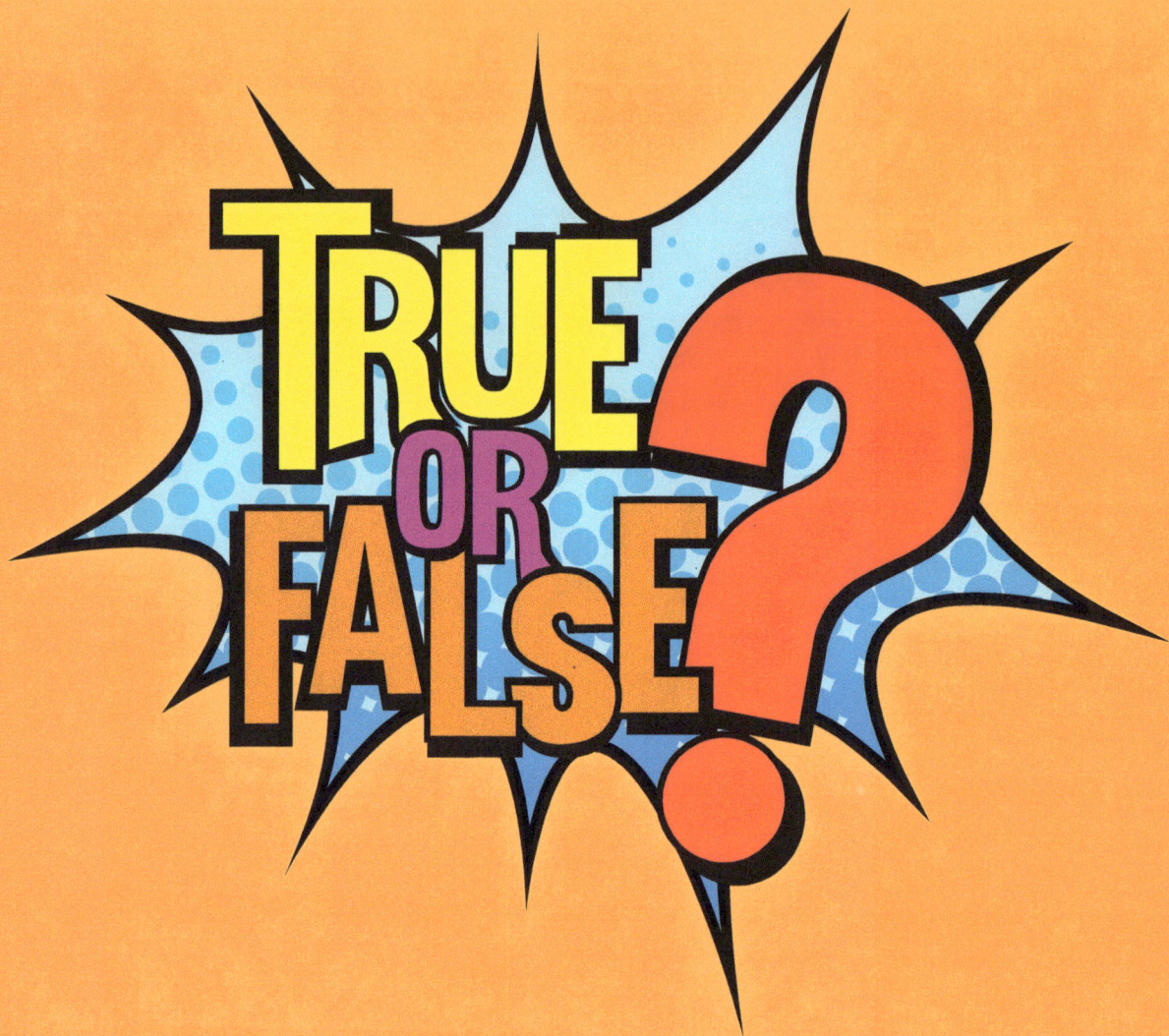

The Warner Bros. studio had an immediate hit with Bugs Bunny, winning the Academy Award for best animated short three years in a row, starting in 1940.

49

FALSE!

Bugs did not win his first Academy Award until 1958, with the short film "Knighty Knight Bugs." Bugs was obviously unable to attend, so the producer John W. Burton accepted the award in his place.

TRUE OR FALSE?

Even though the Walt Disney Company and Warner Bros. are competitors, characters from both studios appeared in a motion picture together.

TRUE!

Bugs Bunny, Mickey Mouse, and other classic characters appeared in the animated mystery *Who Framed Roger Rabbit?* (1988). The dark comedy presented a grown-up take on cartoon characters, combining live action with animation.

TRUE OR FALSE?

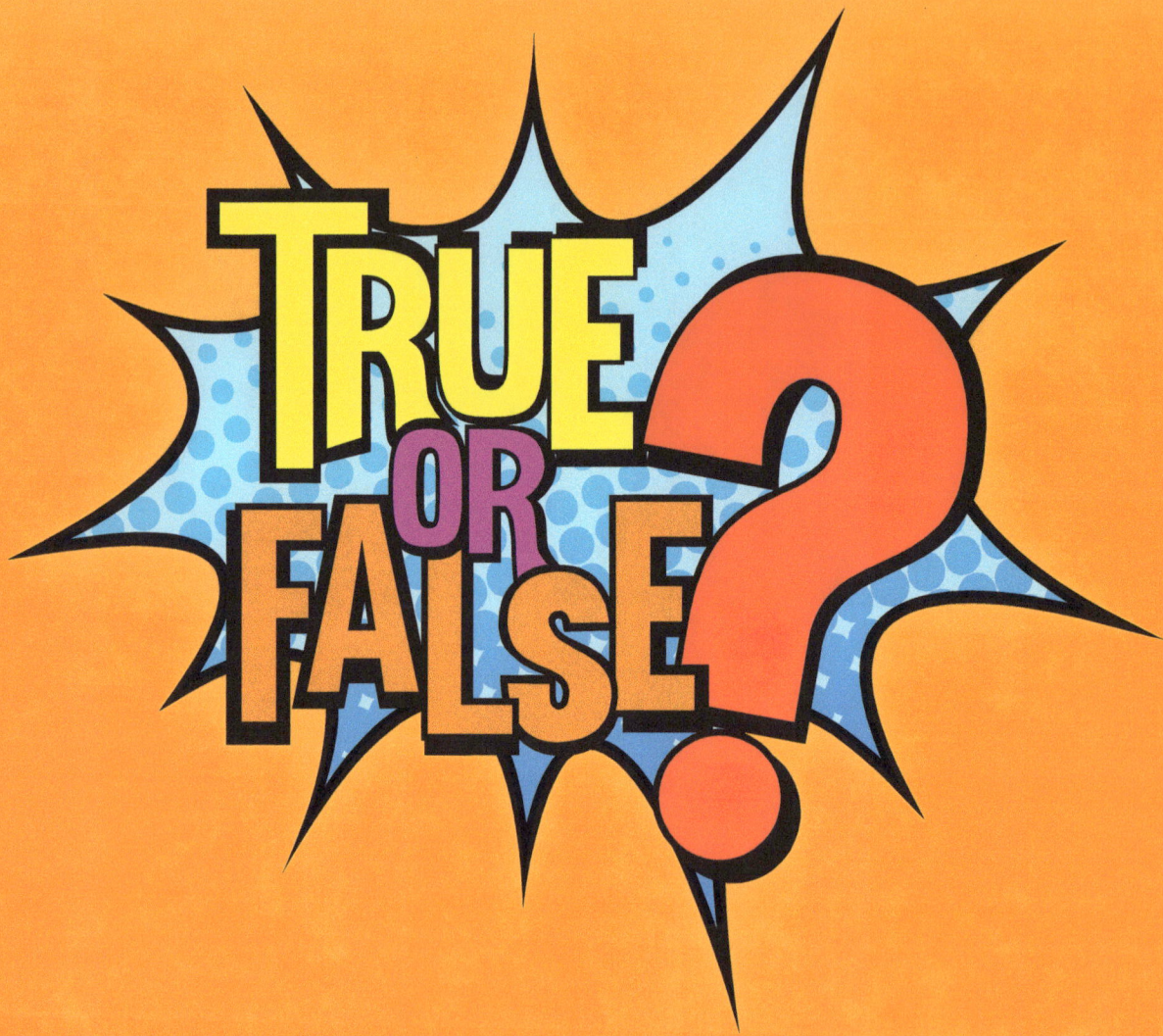

With modern computers, directors can upload a few drawings showing how they want their motion picture to look. The computer does the rest.

(medium - close up)

Even with modern computers, creating a major motion picture requires a team of professionals. More than 100 animators may work together to make sure that everything comes out looking just as the director imagined.

TRUE OR FALSE?

Animation is also used in "live-action" movies.

TRUE!

Blockbuster movies of the past used a lot of real locations and *practical*—that is, noncomputer-generated—special effects. But newer films use computer-generated imagery (CGI) to show everything from dinosaurs to distant planets.

TRUE OR FALSE?

LeBron James was not the only real-life basketball player to appear in *Space Jam: A New Legacy* (2021).

TRUE!

The professional players Diana Taurasi, Nneka Ogwumike, Anthony Davis, Klay Thompson, and Damian Lillard all voice toon versions of themselves.

TRUE OR FALSE?

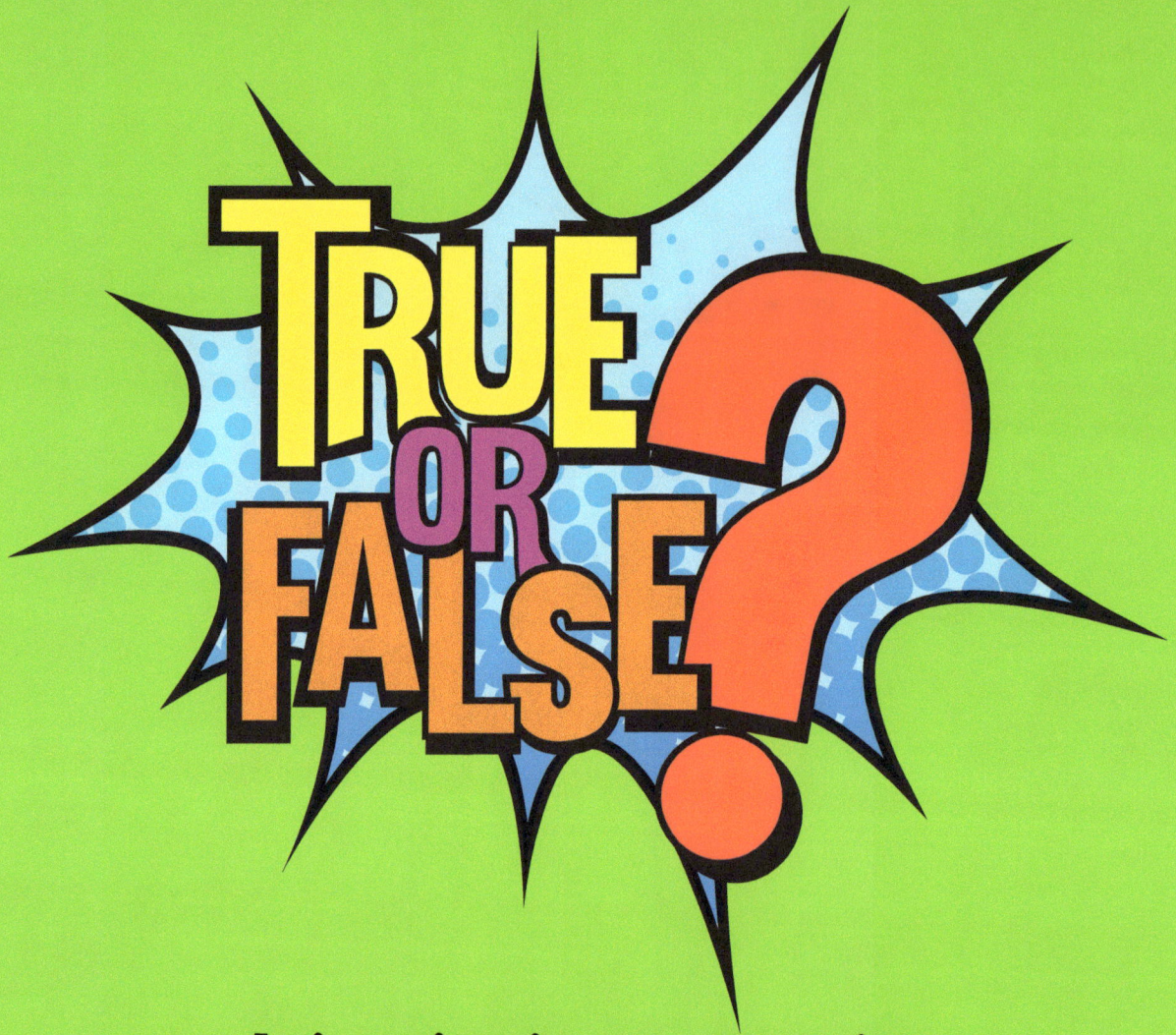

Animation is so expensive and complicated that only big movie studios can make animated movies.

FALSE!

You can make a kind of animation called *stop motion* using toys and a mobile phone camera. Stop-motion animation is created by taking photographs of objects. The objects are repositioned slightly in each photograph. Showing the photographs in order creates the illusion of motion.

TRUE OR FALSE?

Despite their popularity, animated movies have never been nominated for an Academy Award for best picture.

FALSE!

The Walt Disney Company's 1991 movie *Beauty and the Beast* became the first animated film nominated for best picture. Best picture nominations were later given to *Up* in 2009 and *Toy Story 3* in 2010.

TRUE OR FALSE?

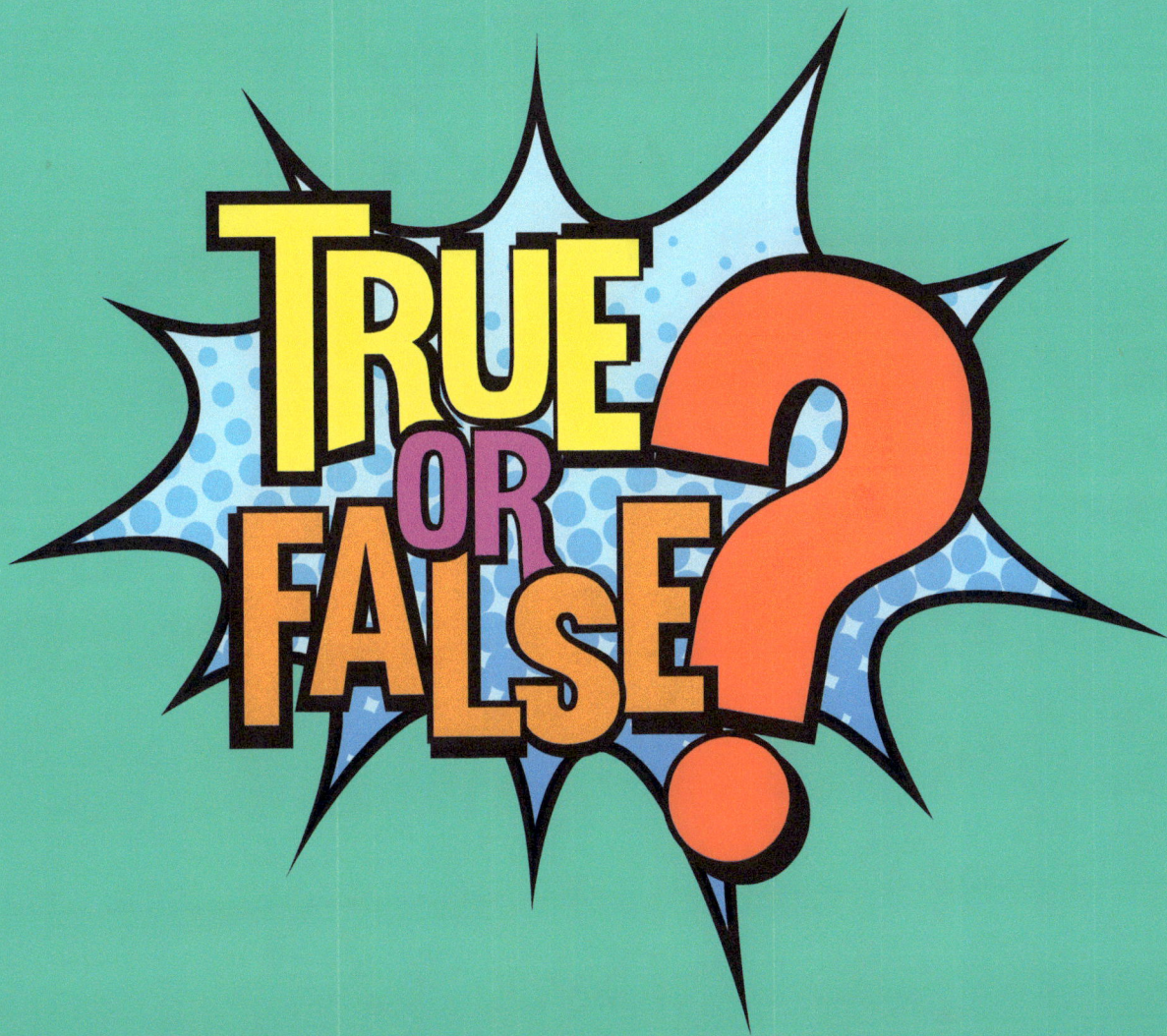

Toy Story (1995) was the first full-length animated motion picture made entirely using computer-generated imagery (CGI).

TRUE!

Buzz, Woody, and the rest of Andy's toys were brought to life on computer by animators at the Walt Disney Company and Pixar Animation Studios. In 2012, two *Toy Story* superfans recreated the film using actual toys.

TRUE OR FALSE?

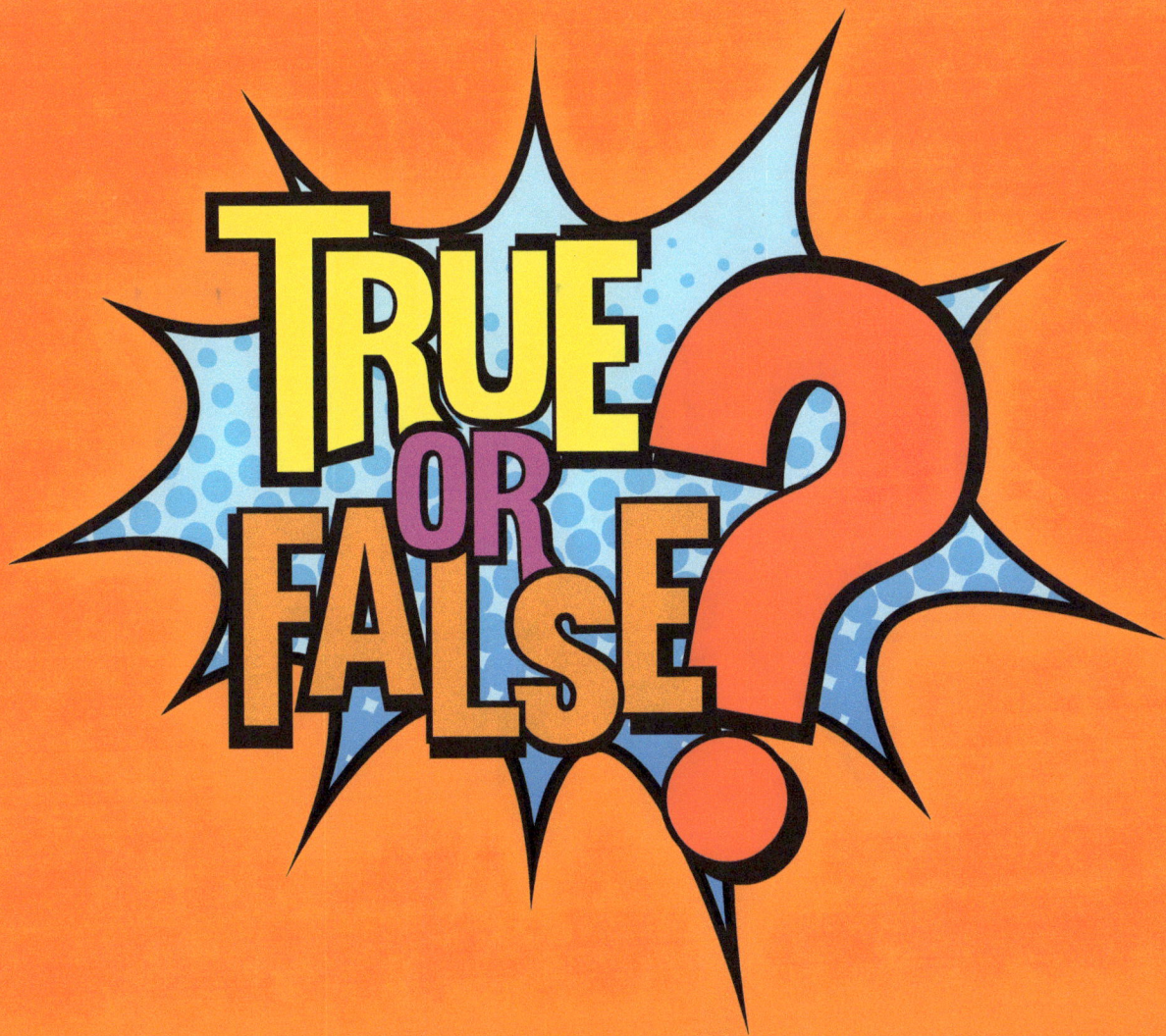

Anastasia Romanov, the subject of the 1997 animated film *Anastasia*, is one of the characters you can meet at Disneyland Paris.

FALSE!

The film *Anastasia* was made by the studio 20th Century Fox—not Disney— and directed by the animator Don Bluth. Bluth directed many animated classics, including *The Land Before Time* (1988) and *All Dogs Go to Heaven* (1989).

TRUE OR FALSE?

The animated motion picture *Encanto* was originally completed in 2019, but it was not released until 2021 due to the COVID-19 pandemic.

FALSE!

Work did not even begin on *Encanto* until the summer of 2020. With workplaces closed to prevent the spread of illness, the animators and crew worked from their homes, communicating by video chat.

TRUE OR FALSE?

To bring *Encanto* to life, animators invested much research into the history, culture, and even plants of Colombia.

TRUE!

The animators worked with a team of Colombian experts to make sure that every detail—down to plants in the magical Madrigal family's home— was true to the setting.

DID YOU KNOW...

The character Elsa was originally meant to be the villain of the movie *Frozen* (2013). After hearing her anthem "Let It Go," however, the creators decided to **make her one of the heroes.**

Animators love leaving little **"Easter Eggs"**— hidden images or other secrets— for people to find in their films. Disney movies are filled with hidden Mickey Mouse symbols, and the studio Pixar often leaves clues to upcoming movies.

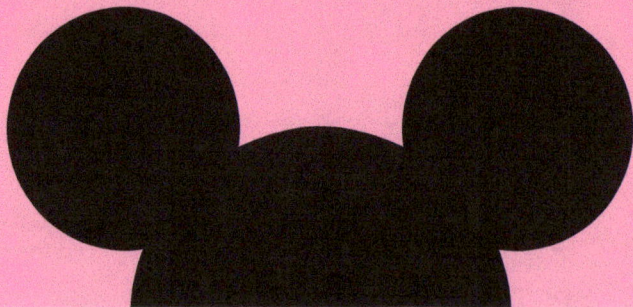

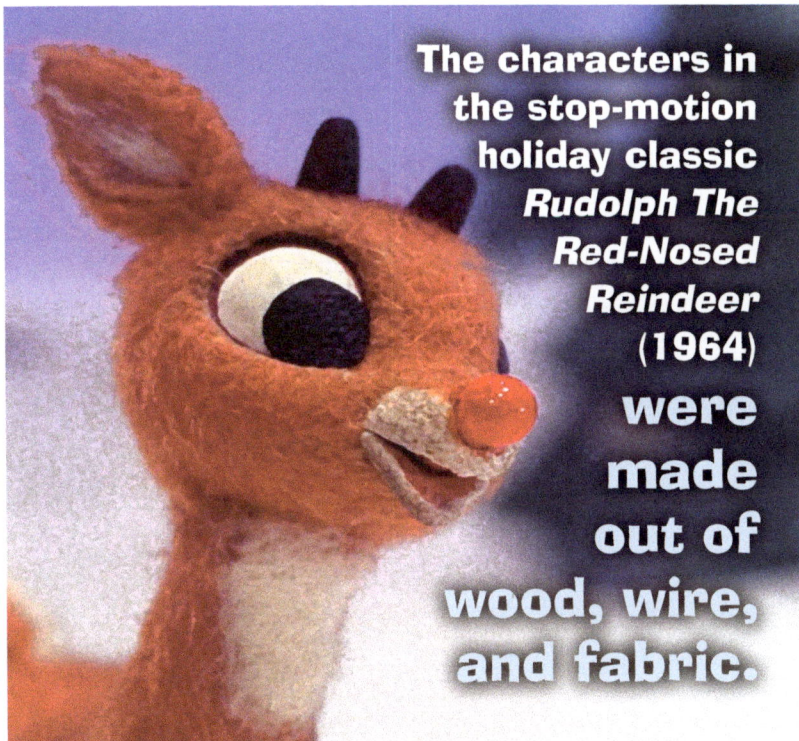

The characters in the stop-motion holiday classic *Rudolph The Red-Nosed Reindeer* (1964) **were made out of wood, wire, and fabric.**

The stop-motion animated film *Marcel the Shell with Shoes On* (2021) began as a series of short films on the video-sharing site **YouTube.**

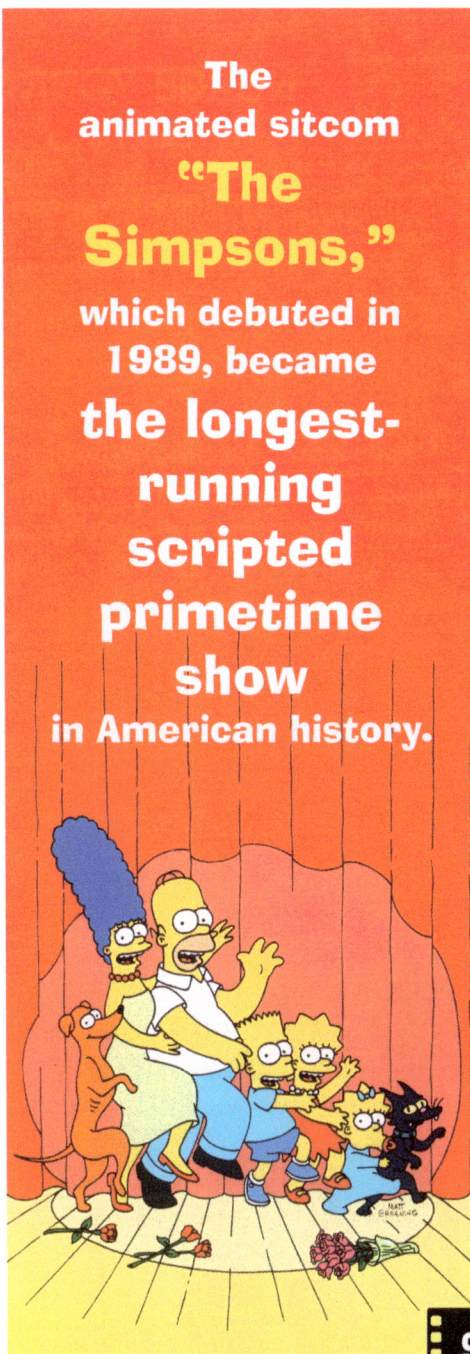

The animated sitcom **"The Simpsons,"** which debuted in 1989, became **the longest-running scripted primetime show** in American history.

93

ENGAGE YOUR READER

GUIDED READING PROMPTS

Before Reading

- Allow readers to scan the text and discuss what they notice so far. Highlight the structure of this text and explain that the answers include both evidence and reasoning that support the claim of true or false.
- Explain the literacy skill: *Sometimes authors write a claim and then use evidence and reasoning to help make their point clear. Look for these elements as you read!*

During Reading

- Read each statement and provide time to discuss whether readers believe it to be true or false before turning the page to learn the facts.
- As you read, model how to identify the claims, evidence, and reasoning in the text. Prompt your readers to identify these features as they explore the text, too.
- Encourage readers to further discuss their learning by pausing to discuss surprising information.

After Reading

- Prompt your readers to connect, extend, and challenge their thinking about the text:
    - What will you take away from reading this text?
    - What changes in your thinking happened while reading and learning?
    - What is still challenging your thinking? What questions or wonderings do you still have?

LOOK BACK!

- Prompt readers to look back through the text to identify examples of interesting or thought-provoking claims.
- Challenge readers to explain what makes these examples so engaging.

CURRICULUM CONNECTIONS

These questions and tasks support the following English/Language Arts skills:

- Determining what a text says both explicitly and implicitly
- Citing specific evidence when drawing conclusions
- Interpreting words and phrases used in a text
- Analyzing how the structure of a text affects how it is read.

LITERACY SKILL

Authors make their claims stronger by supporting them with evidence and reasoning.

- A claim is a statement of truth.
- Evidence includes the facts or information that prove whether the claim is true.
- Reasoning includes any logical explanation that describes how the evidence supports the claim.

Example from the text: Pages 56-59

- Claim: Even with modern technology, directors rely on real animators to make large productions.
- Evidence: More than 100 animators may work together to create a major motion picture.
- Reasoning: Computers and technology are not quite advanced enough yet to be as detailed and as accurate as directors want.

EXTEND THROUGH WRITING

Challenge readers to create their own True/False questions and answers about Animation.

- Have readers use a trusted reference, such as www.worldbookonline.com, to research information related to Animation. Encourage readers to look for key details, fun facts, or surprising features that would make strong True or False statements.
- Give readers one notecard for each claim they research.
- Direct readers to write the claim on the front of the notecard. On the back, readers should describe why that claim is true or false using evidence and reasoning from their research.

MORE WAYS TO ENGAGE!

- Play a game! After considering each claim, have readers signify "true" with a thumb up and "false" with a thumb down. Keep score to see who knows their facts about Animation the best!
  - Develop collaboration skills by grouping readers together into teams.
- Further discuss any True/False claims that revealed readers' misconceptions. Focus the conversation on *why* they initially thought what they did and how the text helped them learn.

Acknowledgments

Cover: © BNP Design Studio/Shutterstock;
© Sujono sujono/Shutterstock;
© George Rudy, Shutterstock;
© Arbit/Shutterstock; © Ray Senlye,
Shutterstock

4-5 © Photo 12/Alamy Images
6-9 © Shutterstock
10-11 © Brian J Ritchie, Shutterstock;
© Ani Kirakosyan, Shutterstock
12-15 © Walt Disney Pictures
16-17 © Nickelodeon
18-19 © Andres Otero, Wenn/Alamy
Images
20-23 © Warner Bros. Cartoons
24-25 © Kobal/Shutterstock
26-27 © ABC
28-31 © Shutterstock
32-33 © Allstar Picture Library/Alamy
Images
34-35 © Masheter Movie Archive/Alamy
Images
36-37 © RKO Radio Pictures
38-39 © RGR Collection/Alamy Images
40-45 © Universal Pictures
46-47 © Photo 12/Alamy Images
48-51 © Universal Pictures
52-53 © Romolo Tavani, Shutterstock
54-55 © Buena Vista Pictures Distribution

56-57 © smolaw/Shutterstock
58-59 © Jeff Morgan 06/Alamy Images
60-63 © Sony Pictures
64-67 © Warner Bros. Pictures
68-69 © Walt Disney Studios Motion
Pictures
70-73 © Shutterstock
74-79 © Buena Vista Pictures Distribution
80-81 © 20th Century Fox
82-83 © AJ Pics/Alamy Images
84-91 © Walt Disney Studios Motion
Pictures
92-93 © Shutterstock; © Walt Disney
Studios Motion Pictures; © NBC;
© A24; © PictureLux/The
Hollywood Archive/Alamy Images
94 © ShiipArt/Shutterstock;
© NeMaria/Shutterstock

www.ingramcontent.com/pod-product-compliance
Lightning Source LLC
Chambersburg PA
CBHW061408090426
42740CB00023B/3472